This book is dedicated to all the scientists, engineers, and researchers who have worked tirelessly to make artificial intelligence a reality.

Your hard work and dedication has made it possible for the world to experience the first AI-generated book. Thank you for helping to make this a reality.

THE FIRST AI-GENERATED BOOK

FIRST ARTIFICIAL GENERATED BOOK BY OPENAI ALGORITHM.

SUBHASH CHAUDHARY

Contents

Foreword   *vii*

Preface   *ix*

Acknowledgements   *xi*

Prologue   *xiii*

1. A Glimpse Into The Future   1

2. The Experiment Begins   3

3. The Results Are In   5

Epilogue   7

Foreword

In the ever-evolving world of technology, artificial intelligence has become an essential tool for many people worldwide.

We have seen AI used for everything from medical diagnoses to autonomous driving and even natural language processing. We have taken a giant leap forward by creating the first AI-generated book.

The First AI-Generated Book is a groundbreaking work that pushes the boundaries of what is possible with artificial intelligence.

This book is the first of its kind, utilizing techniques such as Natural Language Generation (NLG) to generate entire stories and narratives from scratch.

By leveraging existing knowledge bases, the AI is able to generate stories that are both unique and entertaining.

The stories in this book are not only entertaining but also thought-provoking. They offer an insight into the possibilities of AI-generated content and the potential for artificial intelligence to create truly unique works of art.

As we continue to explore AI's capabilities, this book serves as an exciting proof of concept that shows the potential of AI-generated content.

We are excited to present The First AI-Generated Book and look forward to seeing how AI-generated content evolves in the future.

Sincerely,
Subhash Chaudhary

Preface

This is the first book written by Artificial Intelligence and it is a landmark moment in the history of literature and technology.

In this book, we explore the story of how one AI program was able to create a book from scratch, using nothing but its own algorithms and data.

We will explore the implications of such a feat, and what it means for the future of literature, technology, and the arts.

We will also take a look at the ethical and moral implications of using Artificial Intelligence to create books, and how this could change the way books are written and read.

Finally, we will discuss the potential applications of AI-powered writing and how it could revolutionize the publishing industry.

This book is a must-read for anyone interested in the advancements of technology, literature, and the arts. It is an engaging, informative, and thought-provoking look at the potential of Artificial Intelligence and the implications of its use in the writing and publishing worlds.

Acknowledgements

I would like to express my deepest gratitude to those who have helped make this book, "The First AI-Generated Book," a reality.

First and foremost, I am grateful to the team of researchers who developed the Artificial Intelligence technology that made this book possible.

Their hard work and dedication to the project have been invaluable in creating a tool capable of generating interesting and unique stories.

I would also like to thank the editors and publishers who have provided support and guidance throughout the writing and editing process.

Their insight and expertise have been invaluable in making this book a success.

Finally, I thank the readers who have taken the time to read and enjoy this book.

Without their willingness to engage with the stories and characters created by AI technology, none of this would have been possible. Thank you all!

Prologue

Once upon a time in a far away land, a group of scientists and engineers had a dream. They dreamed of creating a machine that could write a book.

A book that would be created by artificial intelligence and not a human. This AI-generated book would be a masterpiece of its own kind, a work of art created by a computer. The scientists and engineers worked day and night tirelessly to make this dream a reality.

Finally, the first AI-generated book was born after years of hard work. It was a work of advanced technology and a testament to the power of artificial intelligence.

This book is the story of that first AI-generated book, and all the struggles and successes it faced along the way.

It is a story of a revolution, of a new age in literature, and of a future where artificial intelligence and humans can work together to create something truly unique.

So, without further ado, let us begin our journey into the first AI-generated book.

CHAPTER ONE

A Glimpse Into the Future

The year is 2045, and the world is much different than it was just a few decades ago.

Artificial intelligence has become a standard part of everyday life, both in the form of interactive assistants and autonomous robots.

The first AI-Generated book has been a resounding success, paving the way for many more. In the world of literature, AI-Generated books are now the norm.

AI algorithms have been developed to create entire stories, novels, and even poetry with creativity and nuance that rivals even the most talented human authors.

AI-Generated books are being released regularly, giving readers a seemingly infinite selection of books.

In addition to AI-Generated books, AI-Generated movies, TV shows, and other forms of media have become commonplace.

AI algorithms have been developed that are capable of taking raw footage and editing it together into a cohesive and entertaining work of art.

AI-Generated movies are now winning awards and being celebrated by critics. The human-AI collaboration has also reached unprecedented levels, allowing authors and artists to create works of art that are truly unique.

AI algorithms are being used to generate new ideas, characters, and storylines that can be incorporated into traditional works of art. AI is also being used to help authors refine their stories, tweak characters, and create believable settings.

The possibilities for AI-Generated works of art are seemingly endless. We can now look forward to a future where AI-Generated books, movies, TV shows, and other forms of media are both entertaining and thought-provoking. It is an exciting time for both artists and readers alike.

CHAPTER TWO

The Experiment Begins

The sun had just risen in the sky and the first rays of light shimmered through the windows of the research lab. Inside, scientists and engineers were busy making final preparations for the biggest experiment of their lives. It had been months of planning and preparation, but now the moment of truth had arrived.

After months of coding, tweaking, and testing, the team was finally ready to launch their first AI-generated book. The project had been the brainchild of the team's leader, Professor Jonathan White.

He had wanted to create an artificial intelligence that could generate a unique story using its own ideas and creativity. After months of hard work and dedication, the team finally had a working prototype.

The team had gathered around the console as Professor White began to type in the command to begin the experiment. The computer screen lit up as the program began to execute its instructions.

As the program ran, the scientists and engineers watched in anticipation.

They had worked hard to create this AI and now they were about to witness the results. The AI churned through its instructions, formulating a story from its own knowledge and experience.

After a few minutes, the story began to take shape and the team watched in amazement as the first AI-generated book took life before their very eyes. The experiment had begun.

CHAPTER THREE

The Results are In

After months of hard work, the results of the first AI-Generated book were finally in.

The AI had been trained on a library of stories and novels as well as several genres of writing style.

After careful examination and tweaking, it was able to generate a book that was surprisingly coherent and well-written.

The team behind the AI-Generated book had high hopes for the success of their project and were eager to find out how the public would respond.

As the results started coming in, the team was overwhelmed. Reviews of the book were overwhelmingly positive and the sales numbers were even better.

The book was praised for its originality and clever use of language. Some critics even went so far as to say that the AI-Generated book was better than some of the best-selling novels of the past few years.

The book's success was a dream come true for the team behind it.

Not only did they prove that AI could generate an entertaining and well-written story, but they showed that the public was ready to accept and embrace AI-generated content.

The team celebrated their success and continued to tweak and refine the AI, hoping to replicate the success of the first book.

As they looked back on their journey to get to this point, they were proud of their work and excited to see what the future held.

Epilogue

www.ingramcontent.com/pod-product-compliance
Lightning Source LLC
Chambersburg PA
CBHW032024140726

47988CB00017BA/1704